Harry *and the* Dinosaurs

GULLANE
CHILDREN'S BOOKS

Harry and his dinosaurs
are having a very busy day
hunting for shapes.

Can you help them?

What could it be?

Triceratops
has sniffed out
a square.

What could it be?

Apatosaurus
has found
a triangle.

What could it be?

Tyrannosaurus
and Anchisaurus
have found a
rectangle.

Goodnight dinosaurs!
Goodnight Harry!

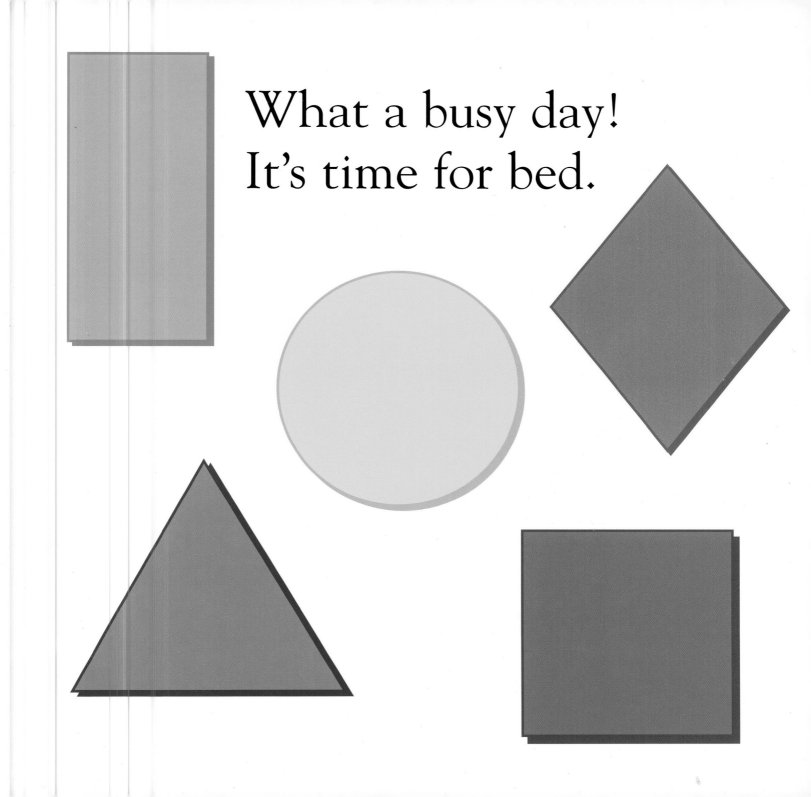

What a busy day!
It's time for bed.

It's Harry's storybook.

rectangle

circle

diamond

square

triangle

rectangle

What could it be?